T0123457

"Whether I shall turn out to be the hero of my own life, or whether that station will be held by anybody else, these pages must show."

—*David Copperfield*, by Charles Dickens

My Dog Ate My Nobel Prize

The Fabricated Memoirs of Jeff Martin

SOFT SKULL PRESS

Library of Congress Cataloging-in-Publication Data is available.

ISBN: 978-1-59376-257-5

Book design and illustrations by Jon Adams
Printed in the United States of America

Soft Skull Press
New York, NY

www.softskull.com

Author's Note

Some of the events described almost happened as related, others were expanded and changed. Others were stretched from the smallest inkling of truth. Others were stolen from other memoirs. Others were found on napkins in diners. Others were completely made up from start to finish. Some of the individuals portrayed are composites of more than one person. Some of these places and people don't exist in any form whatsoever. Many names and identifying characteristics have been changed as well. But it's all true.

Before We Get Started...

I've been thinking about writing a memoir for quite some time. But who hasn't? It seems like every day some no-name with a checkered past or a crazy family pops up on the bookshelves with his or her tale of eccentric woe. But I've never eaten dog poop from a waffle cone or been involved in an orgy with epileptic dwarves. What makes me so damn special? What have I done that deserves to be chronicled and preserved forever? Nothing. Don't get me wrong, I've done some pretty cool things over the years. But great things? Things that will forever alter the world? Nope.

When I was a kid I thought only famous people were allowed to write memoirs, not regular folks like you and me. To write a memoir or an autobiography (even more serious) you had to be old, rich, and famous. Being infamous could also get you into the club, but it really depended on what deeds led you to attain said infamy, like sleeping with 20,000 women or eating your neighbors.

But something happened along the way. There was a shift. Thanks in part to the work of writers like Mary Karr, Frank McCourt, and other used-to-be-unknowns, the reading public at large began to change. No longer would the "life story" and "slice of life" markets be cornered by the likes of David Niven and Shirley MacLaine. The time had come when the merit of a singular story had finally trumped the privilege of celebrity.

But now, many years into the projected lifespan of this trend, it seems that everyone has a story to tell. And I do mean everyone. I mean, if Madonna's brother has a memoir, why can't I? So with great humility and much deliberation, I've decided that if ever there was a time to throw my hat into the ring, it's now.

With all of the controversy we've seen lately regarding the factual integrity of certain bestselling memoirs, I have decided to write this book in a journalistic third-person. To keep the editorializing down to a bare minimum, the events of my life will be presented in a simple date-and-fact format. It's my hope that from these bits and pieces you will see a larger picture, a mosaic in words that tells one version of the story of my life.

Example:

February 7, 1996

In an attempt to resurrect the all-but-extinct grunge movement, Jeff moves to Portland and forms the band Nerve Jam, a bold musical experiment blending the styles of Pearl Jam and Nirvana. To his surprise and disappointment, it fails to catch on.

Now that's made up of course, but it does give you an idea of what to expect from this little book. As I inch ever closer toward my thirtieth birthday, I am beginning to realize that according to projections and estimations, the first third of my life is over. As you'll see in the following pages, I've had many opportunities to do many amazing things. For the sake of brevity (and possible sequels), some of the most shocking things aren't even in the book, like that time when all of my files, records, documents, and proof of pretty much everything that happens in this book were lost in a random warehouse fire. Big time bummer. Yep, there have been plenty of ups and downs along the way, but I am hopeful that the best and most interesting things are yet to come. I hope you enjoy my life as much as I have.

The Early Years

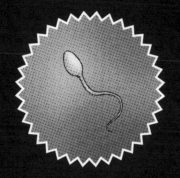

July 19, 1980

Jeffrey Charles Martin is born at St. Francis Hospital in Tulsa, Oklahoma.
He weighs six pounds, thirteen ounces.

Upon seeing the baby, the delivering physician remarks,
"I can't quite put my finger on it, but there is something special about this one."

July 30, 1980

Jeff takes his first steps. His parents are disappointed with his progress; both of his brothers were walking in the first week and running errands to the grocery store within a month. Jeff realizes that he will simply have to work harder than everyone else to achieve the success he desires.

January 20, 1981

At six months of age, Jeff is asked to represent the Society of American Infants (SAI) at Ronald Reagan's first inauguration. Though he was a staunch supporter of the Babies for Carter movement, Jeff decides to put country first and attend the ceremony.

Years later Jeff admits that while he never agreed with Reagan's fiscal policies, the man could give "one hell of a speech."

January 7, 1982

After several unsuccessful attempts, Jeff completes his first novel, *Cossacks Schmossacks*, a lengthy May–December romance set against the backdrop of the Russian Civil War. The book fails to find a publisher. But it does stir enough interest to land Jeff an optimistic agent.

April 26, 1982

Paul McCartney releases the album *Tug of War* but fails to mention Jeff's contribution in the liner notes. It was Jeff, after all, who suggested the song originally titled, "Ivory and Ivory," be changed to "Ebony and Ivory," to promote friendly race relations.

They never speak again.

October 1, 1982

In an attempt to appear like a "real" family, Jeff's parents take him to the opening of the Epcot Center at Walt Disney World in Orlando, Florida. While the park itself is only mildly entertaining, Jeff meets Michael Eisner near the Italian section of the World Showcase, salvaging the trip. The two hit it off instantly and form a friendship that forever changes the course of Jeff's life.

February 28, 1983

The last episode of *M*A*S*H* is destined for failure, but Jeff will not let this happen. He determines to work the pre-show "ground game"—a phrase he coined that night—on very short notice.

His strategy: Calling nearly every nursing and retirement home in America, spreading the rumor that *The Lawrence Welk Show* would be returning to air for one night only.

The *M*A*S*H* finale becomes the most watched program in the history of television; 125 million viewers tune in to say goodbye to the characters they've come to know and love.

When attempted from that day on, this tactic is often referred to as a "Martin," as in "Maybe we should get the ground game going with a Martin" or "I think someone at NBC is trying to pull a Martin on us."

September, 22 1984

Michael Eisner is named CEO of the Walt Disney Company.
One of his first executive actions is to call Jeff and invite him to work with him
on turning around the struggling animation department. While having no
experience in animation, Jeff is a big fan of Saturday morning cartoons.

The first (and only) project that Jeff actually gets his hands on is a film
called *The Black Cauldron*. By the time Jeff gets involved, the film has been in
development for quite some time. With a slated release date of July 24, 1985,
Jeff doesn't have much time to overhaul the project. He quickly cuts the film's
running time from three hours to a more reasonable eighty minutes.

July 24, 1985

The Black Cauldron is released and flops. It goes on to become the most unpopular animated film in the history of the company.

Jeff leaves the Walt Disney Company.
His relationship with Eisner is never reconciled.

Sept. 5, 1985

Jeff begins kindergarten at Herbert Hoover Elementary.

Two weeks later he starts collecting signatures for a petition to rename the school. He argues that no student could truly succeed in a learning institution named after one of our worst presidents.

When the issue is presented to the Board of Education, a compromise is reached. From that day forward the school would simply be called Hoover Elementary.

It is Jeff's hope that people will assume the school is named after W.H. Hoover, founder of the vacuum cleaner empire, and thus associated with the industrialization of cleanliness.

January 28, 1986

The Challenger space shuttle explodes over the Atlantic Ocean killing everyone on board including Christa McAuliffe, a teacher from New Hampshire.

Jeff watches this tragic event live with his classmates. Almost immediately, Jeff decides to carry on in their memory and become the first child in space.

In a move his friends and family call "risky," he drops out of school and moves to Houston. Knowing that he will have to work his way up, Jeff takes a job in the mailroom at the Johnson Space Center. Far too young to legally obtain a work permit in Texas, he convinces everyone that he is a midget.

June 1986

James Cameron calls Jeff with a problem. Set to release his sequel to Ridley Scott's 1979 classic *Alien*, Cameron is stuck on the title. With a bland working title of *Alien 2: More Alien*, the studio is pressuring Cameron to come up with something better. A reporter for *Vogue* was following Jeff at the time, and captured the conversation:

> CAMERON: *"What would it take to get your help on this one?"*
> JEFF: *"You know I'd like to help you Jim, but I'm not in the game anymore and I don't know anything about aliens."*
> CAMERON: *"Wait, what did you just say?"*
> JEFF: *"I said I don't know anything about aliens."*
> CAMERON: *"My God, that's it! Thanks, dude!"* [dial tone]

Alien 2: More Alien goes on to be one of the biggest hits of 1986. It was even supported in the ground game by South Carolina Senator Strom Thurmond. (Though it is widely rumored that he misunderstood the film as a treatise on the ever-growing issue of illegal immigration.)

December 10, 1986

In one of Jeff's more embarrassing moments, he is invited to Stockholm, Sweden, to present famed Holocaust survivor Elie Weisel with the Nobel Peace Prize. Throughout the ceremony he continually mispronounces the last name as "Weasel," not knowing it is pronounced "vee-Zell." He would later admit that he was severely jetlagged and was called in as a last minute replacement for Alan Thicke. The media is relentless.

March 12, 1987

On a visit to New York to see the opening of *Les Miserables* on Broadway, Jeff runs into Mark Johnson, an old friend from his Disney days. Mark has recently left the animation business for a lucrative career as a broker on Wall Street. Over the next few months, Mark helps Jeff invest his money and build a fairly extensive portfolio. The money begins rolling in at breakneck speed. Entire weekends are lost in clouds of cocaine.

October 19, 1987

On what would later be known as "Black Monday," the Dow Jones Industrial Average falls twenty-two percent. Jeff is financially ruined. He never sees or hears from Mark again. The phone stops ringing. Women are no longer interested. In a desperate move to avoid complete poverty, Jeff moves back to Tulsa to live with his parents.

Things are not much better on the home front.
Jeff's once enviable social life is now replaced with a never-ending string of household chores.

February 29, 1988

Nearly a month in the making, Jeff's baking-soda volcano fails to win a prize at the Hoover Elementary Science Fair. This being the latest in a growing string of setbacks, Jeff determines to get his life back on track.

Note: First prize was awarded to Jenny Chang for finding a way to make vegetables taste like candy. Jeff knew he was beaten the moment he tasted her spinach.

June 1–August 29, 1988

With second grade complete, Jeff feels it's time to refocus his attention on something larger than himself. His parents decide to separate. His father takes an apartment while his mother moves into a small house on the street where his grandparents live. On June 1st, Jeff is offered a public relations job with Michael Dukakis's presidential campaign. Welcoming a change of scenery, he moves to Massachusetts immediately.

Over the next few weeks he works harder than ever. Jeff's main area of focus is national security. In most social issues, Dukakis beats Bush hands down. But in the area of national defense and strength, he trails significantly. Throughout the summer Jeff exhausts every idea to build Dukakis's resume and work the ground game with great photo ops. He knows that in politics perception is everything.

With third grade about to begin, Jeff leaves the campaign on August 29th and returns to Tulsa. Before he leaves the campaign he makes an appointment in September for Dukakis to appear at the General Dynamics plant in Michigan for a photo op in an M1 Abrams tank.

Things don't go so well.

September, 1988

With his best interest in mind, Jeff's parents get back together.

They rent a three-bedroom house on an idyllic tree-lined street.

Jeff enrolls at Andrew Carnegie Elementary and begins third grade.

The school's namesake seems like an upgrade from that rotten Herbert Hoover.

However, while doing research for an article in the *Washington Post*, Jeff learns

of the tragic Johnstown Flood of 1889. He discovers that despite his respectable

philanthropic deeds, Carnegie had issues as well. In light of this development

Jeff decides to find at least one politician or public figure with a reputation clean

enough to name a school after. His search continues to this day.

Things at home are good for a while, but Jeff knows that it's only temporary.

January 24, 1989

In the late afternoon, just home from school, Jeff answers the telephone. The operator asks if he accepts a collect call from Florida. He does. Seconds into the call both Jeff and the caller realize that they don't know each other.

> JEFF: *I'm sorry but I think you have the wrong number, Sir.*
> CALLER: *Isn't your area code 818?*
> JEFF: *No, it's 918.*
> CALLER: *Oh, Jesus. Well I am only allowed one phone call and they seem to have dialed incorrectly. Shit.*
> JEFF: *Well, have a nice day…*
> CALLER: *Wait, kid, wait! You don't understand. This is the last phone call I'm ever going to make. Can't we at least talk about something?*

The phone call continues for nearly twenty minutes and covers many topics from classical music to math homework. Jeff doesn't realize until watching the news the next morning that he had been speaking to none other than Ted Bundy.

May 7, 1989

In order to give himself more time to do the things he loves, Jeff leaves Carnegie and decides to take the high school equivalency test. During the test he meets a girl who is also leaving school in order to go to China and help in the ongoing human rights struggle.

Ready for a new adventure, Jeff asks if he can join her. She agrees.
One week later they fly to Beijing.

June 5, 1989

Three weeks into his visit to China, Jeff is on his own. Low on money and cursing the succubus who stole his dictionary, he is lost in a country on the brink of chaos.

While wandering the streets in search of a new English-Mandarin dictionary, he sees a long line of tanks rolling toward him. Remembering what his mother always said—"If you're ever lost, find a police officer or a man in uniform"—he decides to ask directions from one of the men in the tanks. He waves for a moment but they pay no mind. Determined to get their attention, he stands directly in front of the tanks until they stop. He then proceeds to climb up onto the tank and ask the driver for directions to the nearest bookstore.

Coincidentally, the driver happens to have an old English-Mandarin dictionary with him, which he gives to Jeff for nothing in return.

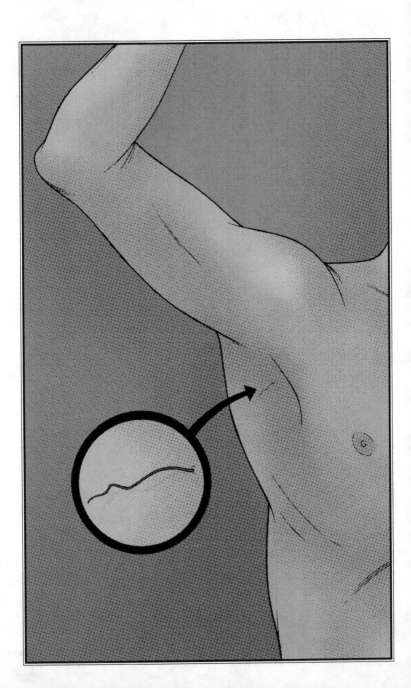

November 6, 1989

Nearly a year to the day after her husband's defeat in his run for the presidency, Kitty Dukakis is hospitalized for drinking rubbing alcohol. When Jeff hears this news he remembers a time when Mrs. Dukakis asked him to run down to the local drug store to buy several bottles of said substance. He has always assumed she was removing an unusual amount of price stickers.

The guilt is overwhelming.

Meanwhile, he discovers he has grown an armpit hair. It is a bittersweet, watershed moment in his youth.

The Nineties

January 7, 1990

On the last day of his annual holiday trip to Italy, Jeff decides to visit Pisa and see the famous Leaning Tower. However, when he arrives, he is told that it is closed due to safety concerns. He is not pleased.

What follows is this conversation, in Italian, with a tower guard…

JEFF: *Perché è la Torre chiuso? (Why is the tower closed?)*
GUARD: *Non so. (Don't know.)*
JEFF: *Perché? (Why?)*
GUARD: *Questo è il mio primo giorno. (This is my first day.)*
JEFF: *Sei stupidi? (Are you stupid?)*
GUARD: *No, io Bernardo. (No, I am Bernardo.)*
JEFF: *Ciao, Bernardo. (Goodbye, Bernardo.)*

What follows is his conversation with himself moments later…

"How can it be closed? It's already leaning, obviously there are some structural problems here. That's like saying 'Don't touch the Liberty Bell, you might break it.' Oh great. I think I just stepped in dog shit."

September 18, 1990

After years of handing out flyers and pamphlets promoting better U.S.-Liechtenstein relations, Jeff receives a fax informing him that Liechtenstein has finally become a member of the United Nations.

Later in the evening he admits to friends that he was beginning to lose hope.

He spends most of the night trying to find someone from Liechtenstein to celebrate with, but settles for an elderly woman who once visited a small Austrian town near the Liechtenstein border.

October 15, 1990

Jeff moves to Seattle at the urging of his friend Bruce Pavitt, co-founder of the independent record label, Sub Pop. Things are going well for the "little label that could" but Pavitt knows Jeff's reputation as a no-nonsense manager. He enlists Jeff to "trim the fat" and find a way to focus on fewer bands with bigger potential.

On his first day in the office Jeff terminates the contracts with seven bands, including Nirvana, whose first album, *Bleach*, had underperformed in Jeff's eyes.

He ventures to Iraq on a talent-scouting mission.

March 5, 1991

Jeff, along with fifteen other Americans, is released from a POW camp in Iraq. He was captured on February 20th while scouting new bands on the outskirts of Baghdad. His idea to put on a post-war benefit concert called "Iraq and Roll" is put on hold while he is incarcerated.

He returns home unharmed but with plenty of "kick-ass" demo tapes.

June 17, 1991

In his first serious financial move since 1987, Jeff decides to buy eight percent of the Vermont Flannel Company, noticing the clothing trends brought on by the burgeoning grunge movement.

He calls his old friend Cameron Crowe, who is prepping to make a film set in and around the grunge world, and suggests he buy the flannel for his actors through the Vermont Flannel Company.

Cameron Crowe has no idea that Jeff owns eight percent of the company.

Two months later the Warner Brothers wardrobe department orders 600 flannel button-ups.

September 24, 1991

Nirvana releases their second album *Nevermind* on the DGC label, a subsidiary of Geffen Records.

The next day Jeff is relieved of his duties at Sub Pop.

January 11, 1992

Jeff travels to South Africa to join Paul Simon as he kicks off his tour. He is the first major artist from the U.S. to play in the country since the United Nations lifted its cultural boycott. Near the end of the performance, Paul convinces a reluctant Jeff to join him onstage. They reenact the music video for Simon's hit song "You Can Call Me Al" with Jeff taking on the Chevy Chase role.

March 31, 1992

The long-running news program *Dateline* debuts on NBC.
It is widely rumored that Jeff was a close second for the job that eventually went
to Stone Phillips.

When an anonymous network executive is asked why Phillips was chosen he
answers, "We all liked the idea of what Mr. Martin could bring to the show, but
at the end of the day we needed someone old enough to drive himself to work."

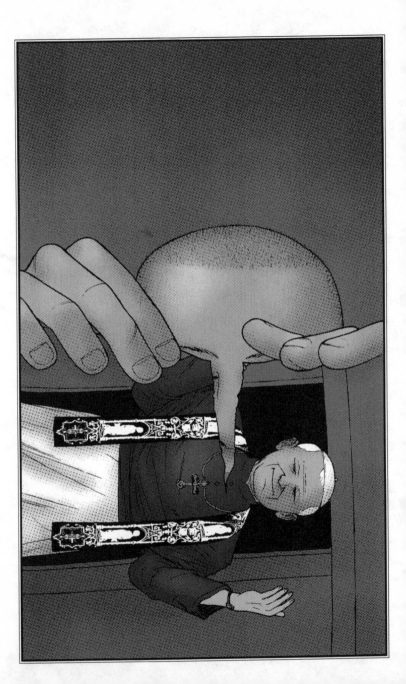

October 3, 1992

While hanging out in the green room at *Saturday Night Live*, Jeff ends up having a long conversation with Sinead O'Connor who is scheduled to perform that night.

SINEAD: *Do you mind if I run something by you?*

JEFF: *No, go ahead.*

SINEAD: *I want to hold up a photo of the Pope tonight when I sing the word "evil" in my song. What do you think about that?*

JEFF: *Why?*

SINEAD: *Because I want to be controversial.*

JEFF: *And that's what you call controversial, holding up a photo? What if someone has the sound turned off? They might think you love the guy.*

SINEAD: *Well, have you got any better ideas?*

JEFF: *As a matter of fact, I do. What if you rip up the photo and then throw the pieces at the camera?*

SINEAD: *Perfect!*

Later in the evening she does just that.

January 14, 1993

Jeff enters a Tucson hospital for "exhaustion." The tabloids have a field day with the topic, even claiming to have photos of Jeff huffing paint behind an Ace Hardware in Little Rock. The photos never surface. Jeff considers legal action, but is too exhausted to follow through.

March 28, 1993

While attending a red-carpet event in Hollywood, a reporter from
Entertainment Tonight asked a visibly intoxicated Jeff his opinion about Bill
Murray's latest film.

ET: *So, what did you think about* Groundhog Day?

JEFF: *Well, I don't really understand the whole shadow thing.*

ET: *No, not the holiday, the movie.*

JEFF: *Is that the one where the guy repeats the same day over and over and over again?*

ET: *Yes.*

JEFF: *To be honest with you I thought it sucked, sucked, sucked. (Burp)*

News of this interview travels fast. Murray isn't pleased.

July 19, 1993

Back living with his mother in Tulsa, Jeff celebrates his thirteenth birthday. A cake is baked. A party is thrown. But Jeff is inconsolable. He is angry at himself. He has fallen victim to the same banal lifestyle as his junior-high friends.

MOM: *Happy birthday, honey! Isn't it exciting finally being a real teenager?*

JEFF: *Lady, I've lived a thousand lives. You think I'm going to get that excited about being a teenager?*

MOM: *Do not call me "Lady"!*

JEFF: *Sorry Mom.*

August 30, 1993

After leaving NBC earlier in the year, *The Late Show with David Letterman* debuts on CBS. Jeff is slated to be a guest on the show but is bumped when Bill Murray refuses to be in the same building with him.

February 12, 1994

Jeff is in Lillehammer, Norway, writing a piece for *Vanity Fair* on the opening ceremony of the Winter Olympics. The festivities don't begin until evening and Jeff has most of the day to explore.

While lunching at a local café, Jeff meets three locals and is invited to join them on a road trip to Oslo. Feeling adventurous, Jeff accepts the invitation on the condition that he be back in time to cover the ceremony.

Upon arriving in Oslo, the men pull up in front of the National Museum. Jeff is asked to stay in the car while his hosts pick up something in the museum gift shop. Moments later the men come running out of the museum screaming at Jeff to start the car.

It is immediately apparent to Jeff that he has just been involved in some sort of theft. What is not apparent, and will only be learned from watching the news the next morning, is that the three men had stolen Edvard Munch's *The Scream*.

He makes it back to Lillehammer in time, but does not include the theft in his piece for *Vanity Fair*.

August 12, 1994

In the spirit of the event, Jeff hitchhikes from Boise to attend Woodstock '94. When he arrives in Woodstock on August 14th, the final day of the concert, he is told that the event "isn't actually in Woodstock."

Unable to hitch another ride, Jeff walks nearly ten miles to the town of Saugerties, New York. By the time he arrives, most of his favorite bands have already come and gone. Instead of Bob Dylan and the Grateful Dead, Jeff is treated to the soothing jam-band sounds of Spin Doctors.

December 12, 1994

Jeff enters the Mount Baldy Zen Center located in the San Gabriel Mountains forty miles east of Los Angeles. Another new arrival to the center is Canadian singer-songwriter Leonard Cohen. Noticing his need for strong male leadership, Cohen takes Jeff under his wing.

The eighteen-hour days are hard at first, but provide Jeff with much-needed structure and discipline. Jeff and Leonard decide to tell each other their deepest secrets in order to be free of them forever.

Cohen is amused by Jeff's secrets, finding them almost endearing in their innocence. Jeff, on the other hand, is shocked to learn that the classic song "Suzanne" was inspired by Suzanne Pleshette of *The Bob Newhart Show*.

March 23, 1995

Jeff leaves the Mount Baldy Zen Center. After deciding to stay in California, Jeff uses his old Disney connections to land a job with Pixar, which is set to release the world's first fully computer-animated film. Determined to redeem himself for the entire *Black Cauldron* debacle, Jeff throws himself into his work like never before.

In an interview with *Wired* magazine, *Toy Story* director John Lasseter waxes poetic about working with Jeff...

"He does so much that it's really hard to put your finger on one specific thing. But here's an example of how Jeff made an impact on the film: As you know, we had Tom Hanks voice the role of Woody. What most people don't know is that Tom was called in at the last minute. The original voice of Woody belonged to Gilbert Gottfried. Just a few weeks before the film's release, Jeff came to me and said he just didn't feel that it was working. So, figuring that it couldn't hurt to try another voice, we called Tom and he agreed to do it. Obviously it was the right choice. Those are the things that Jeff brings to the table on a daily basis."

June 4, 1995

Jeff returns to Tulsa for the first time in nearly two years. His mother and father are divorced and both have remarried. He doesn't tell anyone that he is coming home and spends his first day back driving around town in a haze of nostalgia. He eats lunch at one of his favorite old sandwich shops and catches an afternoon movie in a near-empty theater.

November 22, 1995

Toy Story is released and is immediately greeted with rave reviews and sold-out screenings nationwide. Wanting to go out on top, Jeff submits his letter of resignation to Pixar the next morning.

February 10, 1996

World chess champion Garry Kasparov is defeated by a computer known as "Deep Blue." The same day, Jeff loses $250 trying to win a giant stuffed zebra at the state fair.

One week later Kasparov beats the computer in a rematch.
Jeff never wins the zebra.

July 28, 1996

Jeff goes to the DMV and gets his driver's license.

Just in case, he gets his commercial license and motorcycle license while he's there.

November 18, 1996

Jeff's reputation is severely tarnished when his employer, a well-known ornithologist named Tony Silva, is sentenced to seven years in prison for smuggling parrots. For three months Jeff had been transporting Hyacinth Macaws for Silva. His favorite parrot, Louie, was taken from Jeff's car by government officials. As they took Louie away he sang a song that Jeff taught him when they first met: Sir Mixalot's "Baby Got Back." It wasn't really the ideal song for the situation, but Jeff was overcome with emotion just the same.

Later in the evening, Jeff's sadness is overtaken by an extreme sense of paranoia. He worries that Louie may crack under questioning and tell the authorities about some of Jeff's more lurid activities.

February 23, 1997

Jeff accidentally starts a small fire on the Russian space station, Mir. The Russian government is furious and forces Jeff to spend the rest of his trip in the "time out" corner of the space station.

May 15, 1997

Jeff calls fashion designer Yves Saint Laurent and pitches an idea that came to him during his time in space:

Realizing how bulky and uncomfortable the space suit was, Jeff made some rough charcoal sketches for a new and improved space suit that would blend the creativity of high fashion and the functionality needed for such an item. During this phone call, the seed is planted for what would become Cosmic Couture, the world's first fashion line devoted to space wear.

Jeff even came up with the company's first slogan:

Space. Just because there's a lack of oxygen doesn't mean there has to be a lack of style.

September 6, 1997

The funeral for Diana, Princess of Wales, is held at Westminster Abbey. During the ceremony, Elton John performs a reworked version of his classic song "Candle in the Wind" with lyrics changed to reflect the life of Diana instead of Marilyn Monroe. Jeff is relieved to hear this selection. While at Elton's house the night before, Elton told Jeff that he was torn between two songs.

One was the new version of "Candle in the Wind," and the other was a new version of "The Bitch is Back" called "The Bitch is Dead."

Jeff knew that Elton meant "bitch" as a term of endearment, but didn't feel that it would be understood by the guests at the funeral or the people watching around the world. Elton is grateful for Jeff's advice.

January 27, 1998

First Lady Hillary Rodham Clinton calls the threats against her husband a "vast right-wing conspiracy."

Jeff is working for a public relations company in Memphis that represents Kentucky Fried Chicken. Later that afternoon he pitches what would become the famous "Left Wing, Right Wing" Buffalo wing campaign.

He even came up with the first verse of what would become the popular "Left Wing, Right Wing" jingle…

Gun control and right to life
Causes awful lots of strife,
Making peace and hugging trees
Won't defeat our enemies,
There is no way to solve these things
So just sit down and have some wings.
They're delicious!

May 4, 1998

A federal judge in Sacramento, California, gives "Unabomber" Theodore Kaczynski four life sentences plus thirty years after Kaczynski accepted a plea agreement sparing him from the death penalty. Jeff writes a letter to the judge:

Dear Judge,

In light of your recent sentencing of Theodore Kaczynski, I feel you may have been too hard on the man. Of course there is no excuse for the horrible things he did, but he is clearly not functioning with normal mental facilities. I ask that you reconsider your decision. Instead of four life sentences plus thirty years, I suggest you decrease it to just four life sentences. By that time, this man will have paid his debt to society and will have the thirty years to go out in the world and be a human being again. It's just the right thing to do.

Sincerely,
Jeff Martin, Concerned Citizen

November 3, 1998

Former pro wrestler Jesse "The Body" Ventura is elected Governor of Minnesota.

Upon hearing this news, Jeff decides to form an exploratory committee to decide if he should run for congress in 2000. The committee begins to check Jeff's background for possible problems and comes up with something late that evening. Full details are never released, but the *National Inquirer* reported it as something involving a banana, piano wire, and a Margaret Thatcher mask. He is quoted in the article, explaining, "I don't know what you're talking about, but if I did anything controversial last weekend, it's only because I was on a lot of coke. I mean a lot of coke." Jeff's political career is over before it begins.

February 1, 1999

Making his debut as an on-air personality, Jeff helps launch North Dakota Public Radio, in Fargo. His sixty-minute lunchtime talk show, *Prairie Dog Dan's Really Big Show and Variety Hour* is an instant hit. He hears from both of his listeners nearly every day.

June 1, 1999

Jeff leaves North Dakota Public Radio when his attempted contract renegotiation falls through. The station management loved the show but they were unwilling to pay Jeff more for a program with only two listeners statewide.

> JEFF: *Well maybe North Dakota isn't the right place for Prairie Dog Dan.*
>
> STATION MANAGER: *Well, we own the rights for the show, so it will air here with or without you.*
>
> JEFF: *But you can't do—*
>
> STATION MANAGER: *Listen, I'll be real honest with you. You're a nice guy.* But none of us ever understood this whole Prairie Dog Dan thing. If that was a character you played, that's one thing. But you're always you. And you spend most of each show talking about why there was no real need for two Dakotas in the first place.
>
> JEFF: *Well, fine. I already have a job waiting for me in San Antonio.*
>
> STATION MANAGER: *Okay.*
>
> JEFF: *I guess you'll have to say goodbye to Prairie Dog Dan.*
>
> STATION MANAGER: *How can I say goodbye to someone I've never met?*

The next day Jeff leaves for San Antonio, Texas.

September 8, 1999

Jeff attends the memorial service for *Candid Camera* host and creator Allen Funt who had passed away two days earlier. Jeff worked as a production assistant for Funt in the early 1980s and always found him a charming and humble man. As a tribute to the man who helped him get his start, Jeff decides to play a little trick in his honor. He sets up a camera outside his mother's house, knocks on the front door, and the fun begins…

MOTHER: *Oh, hello dear, it's nice of you to stop by. How are things?*
JEFF: *I've got some bad news, Mom. Grandma's dead.*
MOTHER: *Oh my god! [Falls to the ground.] What happened?*
JEFF: *She was refilling the bird feeder when she tripped and hit her head on a rock. The birdseed spilled all over her and a huge flock of birds, well, they pecked her to death.*

The joke goes on for another fifteen minutes until Jeff decides to let the cat out of the bag. His mother is less than thrilled. When he watches the tape that night he agrees that he should have changed the cause of death to something more realistic.

A New Millennium

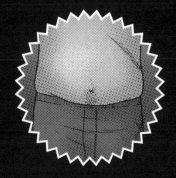

(And Century, and Decade)

January 1, 2000

Jeff spends most of the day at the local Costco returning the nearly ten thousand dollars in supplies he purchased in preparation for Y2K-related chaos.

March 27, 2000

Jeff flies from San Antonio to Moscow where he has been hired to create and direct an outdoor stage show in honor of newly elected President Vladimir Putin. His idea—to bring the glitz and glam of Broadway to Red Square—is met with no small amount of skepticism. But two weeks later, when *Putin on the Ritz* premieres, it is praised by both critics and the new president.

When asked to comment on the show, a clearly beaming Putin exclaims, "Is okay."

November 7, 2000

Jeff votes in his first presidential election.

Results are finalized a mere five weeks later.

In the interim, Jeff forms a political rock group called The Hanging Chads, which consists of four guys wearing Chad Lowe masks and nooses around their necks. Their first and only single, "Lowe Blow" reaches #36 on the Billboard Hot 100.

February 20, 2001

A reluctant Jeff meets with director David Lynch at the Formosa Café in West Hollywood. David wants to hire Jeff as an advisor for his new film *Mulholland Drive*. The two worked together briefly on Lynch's 1990 film *Wild at Heart*, but parted ways after a "creative disagreement." Jeff enjoyed David's films, but found working with such an eccentric personality to be taxing and stressful.

> JEFF: *I'll consider signing on if you can tell me exactly what you want the film to be.*
>
> DAVID: *You know I'm not very good at this, but if it will get you to join us, I'll give it a shot.*
>
> JEFF: *Alright, let's hear it.*
>
> DAVID: *When watching this movie I want the audience to feel like they're driving a milk truck. But instead of milk, they're carrying milk bottles full of rubber cement. No—paste. And they are headed to an abandoned casino in Atlantic City where they'll play poker for three days straight. But they won't use money or chips for betting. I want dried banana slices to take the place of all currency. You know, to say something about the financial system. And, well, I guess the best result would be for someone to walk out of the theater and go "God, I really could go for some yogurt right now." And that's the movie in a nutshell.*

Jeff does not take the job. For his work on *Mulholland Drive*, David Lynch is nominated for an Academy Award.

July 19, 2001

To celebrate his twenty-first birthday, Jeff makes his first trip to Copenhagen, Denmark. He plans to have a calm, quiet stay, but when the workers at his hotel realize that he is checking in on his birthday, they decide to throw him a surprise party. He is flattered by their hospitality and amazed to see a huge table of wrapped presents. His amazement turns to confusion when he begins opening his gifts. One after another, he unwraps different kinds of peppermills.

Some are big, some are small. Some are wooden, while others are metal or plastic. It turns out that in Denmark, if a man is under thirty and unmarried, he is deemed a "pepper man" and is given a multitude of pepper-related products on his birthday.

September 21, 2001

At the request of his friend George Clooney, Jeff takes part in "America: A Tribute to Heroes," a telethon and benefit concert broadcast simultaneously on all four major networks.

Jeff works the phones for most of the evening, speaking to men and women from all across the country. The event raises nearly $30 million for the United Way's September 11th Telethon Fund.

JEFF: *Thank you for calling, how much would you like to pledge?*

CALLER: *Who is this?*

JEFF: *My name is Jeff Martin.*

CALLER: *Are you famous?*

JEFF: *Um, no, not really, but I have done a lot of interesting things in my life,* which eerily coincide with many historical events. Would you like to—

CALLER: *Is Tom Hanks there?*

JEFF: *Well yes, he's in the building, but—*

CALLER: *Let me talk to him instead.*

JEFF: *I don't think that's possible, Sir. Now, can we—*

CALLER: *Listen, I ain't gonna donate shit unless I talk to someone famous.* Got it?

JEFF: *Okay, well, the best I can do is Ray Romano.*

CALLER: *[hangs up]*

February–April, 2002

Jeff moves to New Jersey to work as an advisor to Bruce Springsteen as he completes his new album, *The Rising*. The two met at the 9/11 telethon in New York City and hit it off immediately. The first official E Street Band album in nearly twenty years, *The Rising* is Springsteen's response to that tragic September day. Jeff works tirelessly with the band and producer Brendan O'Brien, even contributing backing vocals to several tracks.

October 22, 2002

After writing a glowing review of the work in the *New York Times*, Jeff is in London to present Canadian author Yann Martel with the prestigious Booker Prize for his novel *Life of Pi*.

One of the key elements in the novel is a Royal Bengal tiger named Richard Parker. In an attempt to liven up the usually stuffy ceremony, Jeff contacts the local zoo and arranges for a similar animal to join him onstage as he presents the award.

The tiger is calm until acclaimed author Salman Rushdie, seated in the first row, makes a sudden move for his wine glass. The tiger then jumps from the stage and proceeds to maul Mr. Rushdie.

The next day an investigation is launched by the British government to determine if the tiger has any Iranian ties.

December 25, 2002

Filling in for the ailing Carrot Top, Jeff travels with the USO to Afghanistan to meet the troops. Under the impression that he has to actually perform Carrot Top's act, he spends two weeks collecting hundreds of props and writing jokes. He is relieved when he finds out otherwise, but also curious to know how well his material would have gone over:

YOUNG WOMAN: *Pardon me, Sir, but do you sequitur?*

MAN: *No, I'm sorry. I quit.*

YOUNG WOMAN: *If I may ask, how long have you been a non sequitur?*

MAN: *Gosh, it must be going on ten years now.*

YOUNG WOMAN: *Wow. Was it hard to quit?*

MAN: *Nope. I used the gum.*

April 12, 2003

While visiting the Des Moines Art Center in Iowa, Jeff meets an up-and-coming young photographer from Boston named Molly Thompson. She is there to shoot a temporary exhibit by Andy Goldsworthy, the British artist famous for constructing impermanent environmental sculptures. When Jeff asks her to explain why someone would spend so much time creating something that won't last, she almost leaves. But Jeff, aware of his mistake, quickly changes the subject.

The two spend the rest of the day together, walking the city streets and talking well into the morning. Molly informs Jeff that she has family in Tulsa and visits often. He likes this news.

October 23, 2003

Back in Los Angeles for the first time in many years, Jeff cuts the ribbon at the opening of the Walt Disney Concert Hall. Designed by his friend and mentor Frank Gehry, the building is a much-needed addition to the LA skyline. At dinner that night, Gehry confides to Jeff that the building's design is loosely based on one of Jeff's sketches from the late eighties. Jeff is flattered. "Well," Gehry explains, "not the sketch itself, but the way the paper looked when you threw it in the trash."

December 9, 2003

Jeff makes a terrible mistake while hosting his weekly radio show on KROQ in Los Angeles. He breaks in during the middle of a song to report that Paul Simon has died.

He gives a touching off-the-cuff speech about the famed musician and plays "Slip Sliding Away." Moments later, the station is flooded with calls. The station manager comes in to inform Jeff that he reported the death of the wrong Paul Simon. The man who died was a former Senator from Illinois, not the singer-songwriter.

He corrects his mistake on the air:

"You're listening to your favorite station, KROQ. Well, I have a slight correction to make. It appears that I may have misspoken when I said that Paul Simon had passed away. I saw the news on Yahoo! and that's what I get for not reading the fine print. Turns out it was some politician, which is sad to many I'm sure, but he probably wasn't a very good guitar player. So once again, Paul Simon is alive and well. And so is Art Garfunkel, not that anyone cares."

February 7, 2004

Jeff and Molly decide to take their relationship to the next level. They move into a two-bedroom brownstone in Brooklyn's Williamsburg neighborhood where Molly works as a staff photographer for *Block* magazine.

Jeff is surprised by the friendliness of his new neighbors.

JEFF: *Is it true that Williamsburg is named for Colonel Jonathan Williams?*
NEIGHBOR: *Go fuck yourself.*

April 29, 2004

Jeff begins rehearsals for his new play, *Horizontal Mambo: A Play About Sex, Not Dancing* at the Atlantic Theater Company in Manhattan. This being his first time writing and directing a play, Jeff sets up a meeting with the theater's co-founder, David Mamet.

Known for being as tough and confrontational as the characters he creates, Jeff is nervous about asking the Pulitzer Prize–winner for advice.

They meet at Gleason's Gym in Brooklyn.

MAMET: *Do you want to be a fuckin' writer?*
JEFF: *Yes I do.*
MAMET: *You want to be a fuckin' writer?*
JEFF: *Yep.*
MAMET: *So you're telling me you want to be a motherfuckin' writer?*
JEFF: *Uh huh.*

August 2004

Jeff is in London working with Woody Allen on rewrites for his new film *Match Point*. Molly is back in the States, unable to be away from work for such a prolonged period. Succumbing to his loneliness, Jeff enters into a brief intimate relationship with Scarlett Johansson.

He considers keeping it a secret forever, but the weight of his deed is too heavy.

> JEFF: *I need to tell you something and it's not going to be easy to hear.*
>
> MOLLY: *What? What is it?*
>
> JEFF: *I, um, I…*
>
> MOLLY: *Just say it already.*
>
> JEFF: *I had sex with Scarlett Johansson.*
>
> MOLLY: *What did you just say?*
>
> JEFF: *I slept with Scarlett Johansson.*
>
> MOLLY: *[laughing hysterically] Yeah right. In your dreams, little man. I've heard some funny things, but that takes the cake.*
>
> JEFF: *Well, there's no fooling you. You got me.*

February 18, 2005

Jeff is kidnapped while in Cairo doing work for the United Nations. Molly calls the U.S. Embassy to inform them that Jeff left to take a walk in the late afternoon and never returned. Hours later, Molly receives a package containing photos of Jeff, bound and blindfolded. She immediately turns the package over to the authorities. Negotiations begin.

June 4, 2005

Jeff is released by his captors and found on a road in rural Belgium. His hair has been bleached and he is missing two toes on his right foot. He is flown back to FBI headquarters for questioning.

FBI: *What can you tell us about these guys?*

JEFF: *I believe they were from the Middle East.*

FBI: *What else?*

JEFF: *They spoke Arabic.*

FBI: *Anything else? What did they look like?*

JEFF: *Brown hair, brown eyes, and lots of beards. Actually, I think everyone had a beard.*

FBI: *Well, why did they cut off your toes?*

JEFF: *They gave me a choice. I could either lose both of my eyebrows or two toes. I started to go with the eyebrows, but then I thought about how weird Whoopi Goldberg looks without them. So it was a pretty easy call to make.*

FBI: *Thank you for your cooperation. With the details you gave us today I think we'll be able to get these bastards. Or at least some guys that look like them.*

November 30, 2005

Jeff and Molly are married by the Reverend Al Green in a small, private ceremony in a chapel north of Montreal. He serenades them with several tunes including "Tired of Being Alone" and "Let's Stay Together." The ceremony is briefly interrupted when the Reverend has a small heart attack while attempting to hit a high note. The remainder of the evening is spent at the hospital.

March 21, 2006

Jeff appears on the Home Shopping Network to launch products for his new company, Green Ink, an eco-friendly pen and ink manufacturer. Sales are fair, but after dealing with several confused callers, Jeff decides to change the company name.

HOST: *I think we have Barbara from Salt Lake City on the line. Barbara, are you there?*

BARBARA: *Yes, hi, thanks for taking my call.*

HOST: *No problem, what's your question this evening?*

BARBARA: *Well, I guess this question is for Mr. Martin. I really love what you are doing for the environment, but do you plan on offering ink in colors other than green?*

JEFF: *Thank you for the kind words. Actually, we are just called Green Ink, but we offer ink in many colors.*

BARBARA: *You mean like different shades of green?*

JEFF: *No, I mean we have blue, black, red, and lots of others.*

BARBARA: *I guess I just don't understand. So you are saying that you will be expanding your colors beyond green at some point?*

JEFF: *Let me explain. The "green" in our company's name represents our environmental policies. It has absolutely nothing to do with the colors of the actual ink or anything like that.*

HOST: *Well, it looks like we lost Barbara. But let me tell you some more about Green Ink…*

July 2, 2006

Jeff has lunch in Bedford, New Hampshire, with inventor and Segway creator, Dean Kamen. Lacking the knowledge and funding to do it alone, Jeff asks Kamen to work with him in the development of a product called "The Piss Bib," a small waterproof cloth that is sewn into the fly of men's pants and pulled out before urination to avoid spillage or splattering.

Kamen is on the fence. But two weeks later Jeff receives a letter from him containing a short note and a check for $200,000.

Dear Jeff,

I have to be honest. When you first told me about your idea I thought it was the dumbest thing I'd ever heard. But a few days later I had a very important meeting in Manhattan. Right before the meeting started I was urinating in the men's room. And I'll be damned if I didn't dribble piss all over the front of my pants. Without a hairdryer or a new pair of slacks to put on, I had to cover my crotch with my briefcase for the next twenty minutes. It was downright embarrassing. So here is a little startup money for some prototypes of "The Piss Bib." All I ask is that you send me a few as soon as they're ready.

Yours,
Dean Kamen

December 17, 2006

Inspired by the scale and ambition of Christo and Jeanne-Claude's *The Gates*, the controversial installation that took Central Park by storm a year earlier, Jeff proposes a project to the city council in which he would wrap the entire Empire State Building with masking tape in order to represent a city in need of constant upkeep and repair.

The motion to accept the project fails by one vote.

July 30, 2007

Legendary Swedish filmmaker Ingmar Bergman dies while shooting a film based loosely on Jeff's childhood. The film, *Youth Interrupted* (Ungdom Avbröt), is permanently shelved. The director became interested in Jeff's story after reading a profile piece in the April 1989 issue of *Esquire*. Stuck in development for nearly two decades, Bergman had finally found a pair of Norwegian investors willing to fund the production. With a relatively small budget of $8 million, principal photography had begun on June 17th. Most of the completed footage was shot in the Swedish city of Lund, which bears an uncanny resemblance to Tulsa in the 1980s.

October 15, 2007

Previews begin for the Broadway debut of Jeff's play, *Horizontal Mambo: A Play About Sex, Not Dancing.* Set for a November 12th debut at the August Wilson Theater on West 52nd, the play is generating a good amount of buzz throughout the New York theater world. One critic even says "Minus some unforeseen disaster, this baby's got 'Tony' written all over it."

November 10, 2007

Two days before Jeff's play is set to open, the stagehands go on strike, causing Broadway to shut down for nearly three weeks. Director Mike Nichols and star Alec Baldwin leave the production to work on various film projects. The play finally makes its debut on December 4th with Jeff taking over directing duties and Tony Danza in the lead role. Reviews are mixed at best.

The show closes two weeks later.

April 5, 2008

Jeff flies to Los Angeles where he auditions to become the new lead singer for the rock band Velvet Revolver. One week earlier, Jeff had received a call from Slash informing him that current singer, Scott Weiland, would be leaving the band on the first of April.

Things go well. Jeff's voice sounds better than ever. At dinner, Slash formally invites Jeff to join the band. Jeff feels strongly that if he comes on board, the band should modify its name to reflect the change. He suggests three similar, but different, band names:

1. Nylon Shotgun
2. Cotton Cannon
3. Fleece Musket

All are rejected.

October 1, 2008

Jeff's first published book, *The Patron is Usually Mistaken: The Service Diaries*, an anthology of essays about the American service industry, is released to great acclaim. Originally meant as a humorous piece of social commentary, the book takes on an unexpected level of relevance due to the worldwide financial crisis.

November 1, 2008

While working on a freelance piece for the *Economist*, Jeff discovers a VHS tape containing footage of Barack Obama jaywalking in 1987. The journalist in him feels compelled to turn the tape over to the Associated Press, but he knows what kind of things the Republicans will try to do with it. Just a few days away from the election, Jeff decides to hold onto the tape until all of the votes are in.

The day after the election, Jeff calls one of his friends at the AP:

FRIEND: *So what's this big important thing you needed to tell me?*
JEFF: *I found a tape.*
FRIEND: *Oh yeah, what kind of tape?*
JEFF: *A videotape from 1987 showing Barack Obama doing something illegal.*
FRIEND: *What? What is it?! Crack? Hookers?*
JEFF: *Jaywalking.*
FRIEND: *Jesus Christ! How long have you had this tape?*
JEFF: *I found it today.*
FRIEND: *Do you know what kind of damage this could have done if it had surfaced before the election? It's a game changer.*
JEFF: *Yeah, I know. Oh well.*

January 27, 2009

With shares at an all-time low, Jeff buys a majority stake in Barnes & Noble, Inc. He appoints himself CEO and considers changing the name of the company to Barnes & Noble & Martin, but the costs associated with new signage and labor prevent him from doing so. In an attempt to increase revenue and cut overhead, Jeff orders that all sprinkler systems be removed from stores immediately.

His argument that "a wet book gets just as ruined as a burned book" baffles many. He does not seem to realize that the sprinklers are in place to save lives and buildings, not books.

Three stores are lost that spring. Luckily, no one is injured.

May 21, 2009

While working for Habitat for Humanity in Seoul, South Korea, Jeff and Molly run into Brad Pitt and Angelina Jolie at Incheon International Airport. Brad and Angelina have just adopted three new children from a dirty, overcrowded orphanage in a bad part of town. But the airline only allows one child per adult. Not wanting to miss their flight or charter an alternative, Brad and Angelina offer one of their new children to Jeff and Molly for $200. Jeff and Molly accept, not wanting to pass up such a good deal. When Jeff and Molly look into the eyes of their beautiful baby girl, they agree that she's worth at least nine to ten times more than they paid.

November 26, 2009

After spending most of the summer painting, Jeff's first exhibition opens at the Gagosian Gallery on Madison Avenue. Twenty of the twenty-five pieces sell within the first half-hour. With a technique that blends the styles of Salvador Dali and Grandma Moses, Jeff takes the art world by storm. The critics at prominent art magazines aren't nearly as kind as the buyers.

"What is this shit?" —*Artforum*

"Huh?" —*Art in America*

"Is it supposed to be funny?" —*New American Paintings*

July 19, 2010

Jeff turns thirty.

As he blows out the candles on his birthday cake, he makes a silent promise to himself to get his act together and really do something with his life.

Appendices

Appendix I

DATES THAT DO NOT APPEAR IN THIS BOOK
FOR LEGAL REASONS

May 1, 1981

April 12, 1983

January 11, 1986

August 10, 1992

December 23, 1996

November 24, 1999

February 9, 2000

March 4, 2005

June 2, 2007

September 30, 2008

Appendix II

TITLES FOR THIS BOOK
THAT JUST DIDN'T WORK

Self-Proclaimed: The Jeff Martin Story

Accidental Achievements

Running with Shears

A Brilliant Life, Brilliantly Lived

The Da Vinci Code

And Then…

A Billion Tiny Fragments

My Life is More Interesting Than Yours

Not Another Holocaust Story

When Animals Attack

Imaginary Accomplishments

Appendix III

10 PEOPLE JEFF WOULD STILL LIKE TO MEET
(please contact Jeff through his website if you have a connection)

Gallagher

Deepak Chopra

Nigella Lawson

Kim Jong-il

Tony Bennett

John Stamos

The Snapple Lady

My real parents

J.D. Salinger's mailman

Brian Boitano

Appendix IV

MOLLY MARTIN INTERVIEWS JEFF MARTIN

MM: *Thank you for agreeing to this interview.*

JM: *Do we really have to be so formal?*

MM: *I'll ask the questions.*

JM: *Okay.*

MM: *Are you planning on taking out the trash sometime this week?*

JM: *Yeah, I'll do it when we get done with this.*

MM: *Great. Now, what about that leak under the sink?*

JM: *Is the whole interview going to be like this?*

MM: *Don't try to change the subject. What about the sink?*

JM: *What about it?*

MM: *Are you planning on fixing it anytime soon?*

JM: *What are these questions?*

MM: *Do you tell Charlie Rose what kind of questions to ask?*

JM: *No. You're right. Go ahead.*

Appendix V

HOW DO YOU FEEL ABOUT
APPEARING IN THIS BOOK?

"Never heard of him." —Michael Eisner

"Did he have big ears?" —Scarlett Johannson

"I never really liked the guy but he did help me out
with that USO gig." —Carrot Top

"He said what?" —Brad Pitt

"Is okay" —Vladimir Putin

"Do I get any royalties from this?" —Paul McCartney

"He ruined my life." —Sinead O'Connor

Acknowledgments

I would like to extend my gratitude and thanks to everyone except Burt Reynolds. You hear me, Burt? I can forgive, but I will never forget. Never.

Highlights from the Upcoming Sequel

My Dog Ate My Nobel Prize…Again:
Even More Fabricated Memoirs of Jeff Martin

December 21, 2012

According to the Mayan calendar, this is the date on which the world is scheduled to end.

It doesn't. Jeff is furious.

He hasn't purchased a single Christmas present. The lines are a nightmare.

July 28, 2061

Having missed its last appearance on February 9th, 1986, Jeff, age eighty-one, is determined to see Haley's comet before he dies.

But just as he is preparing to go outside, he notices that *The Godfather Part II* is about to start on HBO.

He remembers a recent article in *Popular Science* about new advances in longevity and cryogenics.

As crowds fill the streets and the movie begins, Jeff plops down on the couch and says to himself…

"Screw it. I'll catch the next one."

June 7, 2666

A time capsule is unearthed. The contents include a letter written by Jeff Martin from his deathbed.

Below is an excerpt from that letter:

"In my life I had many achievements and did nearly everything I ever set out to do. But one thing I was never able to do was get through Roberto Bolaño's novel 2666. In my nearly 100 attempts, I was never able to get past page thirty-one. I have now been dead for centuries, yet I write to you now, in the far away year of 2666, wondering if this is still an unresolved issue for the citizens of Earth."

The book is now assigned regularly to first-grade students.

A Note About the Type

I usually don't have much to say about fonts and typefaces, but this one has a special place in my heart. A few months back I was sitting in traffic when I saw this font laying in the gutter, drinking a bottle of booze. The last time I'd seen him, he was doing fine. He'd been working for lots of sports magazines and even did a job for *GQ*. But times got tough and now he was living on the street. I don't think he recognized me, and it would have been easy for me to give him a couple of bucks and drive away. But I am glad to say that I made a better choice. I took him to get something to eat, he told me his story, and I offered him a job on this book. Just the other day he rented a little one-bedroom apartment and is starting to get his life back on track.

I don't have the words to tell you what this font means to me, but here's a poem this font once told me:

The quick brown fox jumps over the lazy dog.

About Jeff Martin

Eyes: Brown

Hair: Black

Height: 6'0"

Weight: 165–170lbs (give or take)

Astrological Sign: Cancer

Favorite Color: Mauve

Handedness: Left

Blood type: O

Organ donor: Yes

Printed in the United States
by Baker & Taylor Publisher Services